Hello, Mom

Polly Dunbar

faber

First published as *Hello, Mum* in the UK in 2021
by Faber & Faber Limited
Bloomsbury House
74–77 Great Russell Street
London WC1B 3DA

First published as *Hello, Mom* in the USA in 2022

Printed in India

A CIP record for this book
is available from the British Library

ISBN 978-O-571-36824-2

2 4 6 8 10 9 7 5 3 1

For my boys. x

This book came about quite by accident. I've been writing and illustrating books for children since graduating from art school but it wasn't until I had my own children that I thought about drawing something for grown-ups.

I didn't want all those hilarious and beautiful moments of their childhood to float away like wisps on the wind. It seemed the only way to capture them was a quick doodle; a visual diary, if you like. These drawings were mostly made far too early in the morning, coffee in hand, sketchbook on lap, boys crawling over me "borrowing" my pens.

As well as capturing the sheer exhaustion and utter mayhem of motherhood, I hope I've caught some of the twinkly magic of it all. Children's imaginations have always fascinated me; I guess that's why I write children's books.

I feel very lucky to have my two boys, who show me the world their way, in all its freshness, absurdity and fun.

Thank you to all those who have supported me on social media; it has been hugely encouraging. I'm touched to know that some of you out there relate to these cartoons and feel seen. Of course, thank you to Sonny and Cody, who inspire and wear me out in equal measures - I love you to the kitchen...the moon ...the stars and back again!

Mom, it had
better be
good.
X

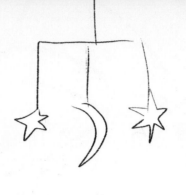

Hello, Baby.

Phase One

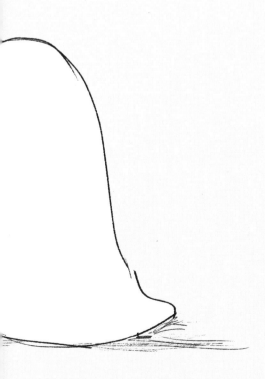

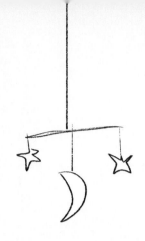

Now what?

How is this possible?

WAAA WAAA WAAA
WAAA WAAA
WAAA
WAAA.

How is this possible!?!

This is impossible.

How is this possible?

How are you so impossibly...

... possible.

Phew.

What's that?

Am I enjoying motherhood?

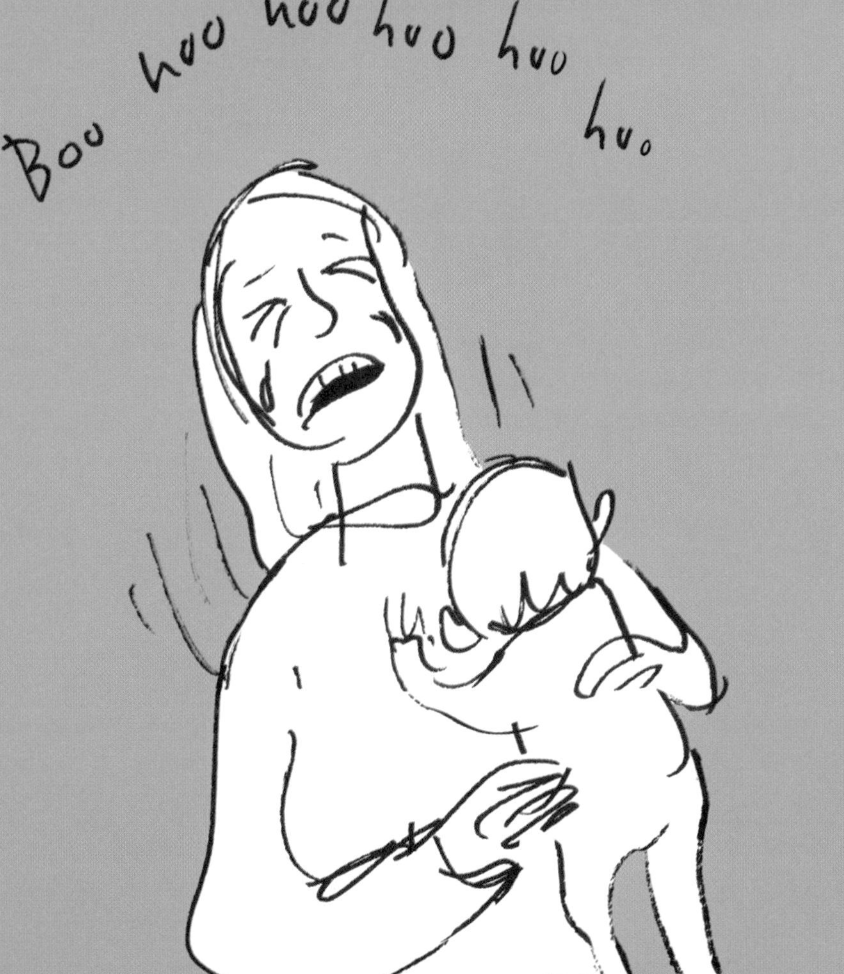
Boo hoo hoo hoo hoo hoo

Yes, of course.

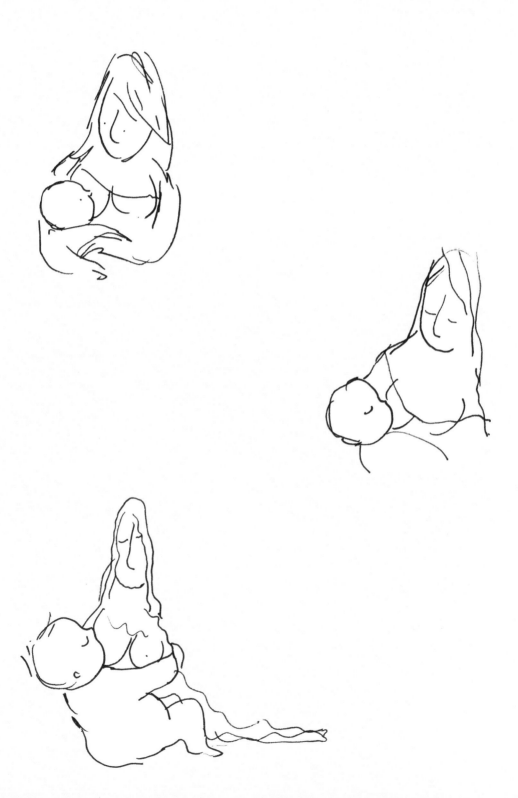

FOLD.

Top of the range,
"fold and go."

Just lift...

...and fold

and fold...

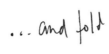

...and fold

and fold...

and fold...

Congratulations!

Folding is complete.

You are good to go!

Oh, you're the loveliest, wuddliest snuggliest, cuddliest thing ever!

Whatever.

Growing up, up, up...

lying

rolling

oh

sitting

oops!

try again...

Crawling

wobbling

Walking...

running...   flying...

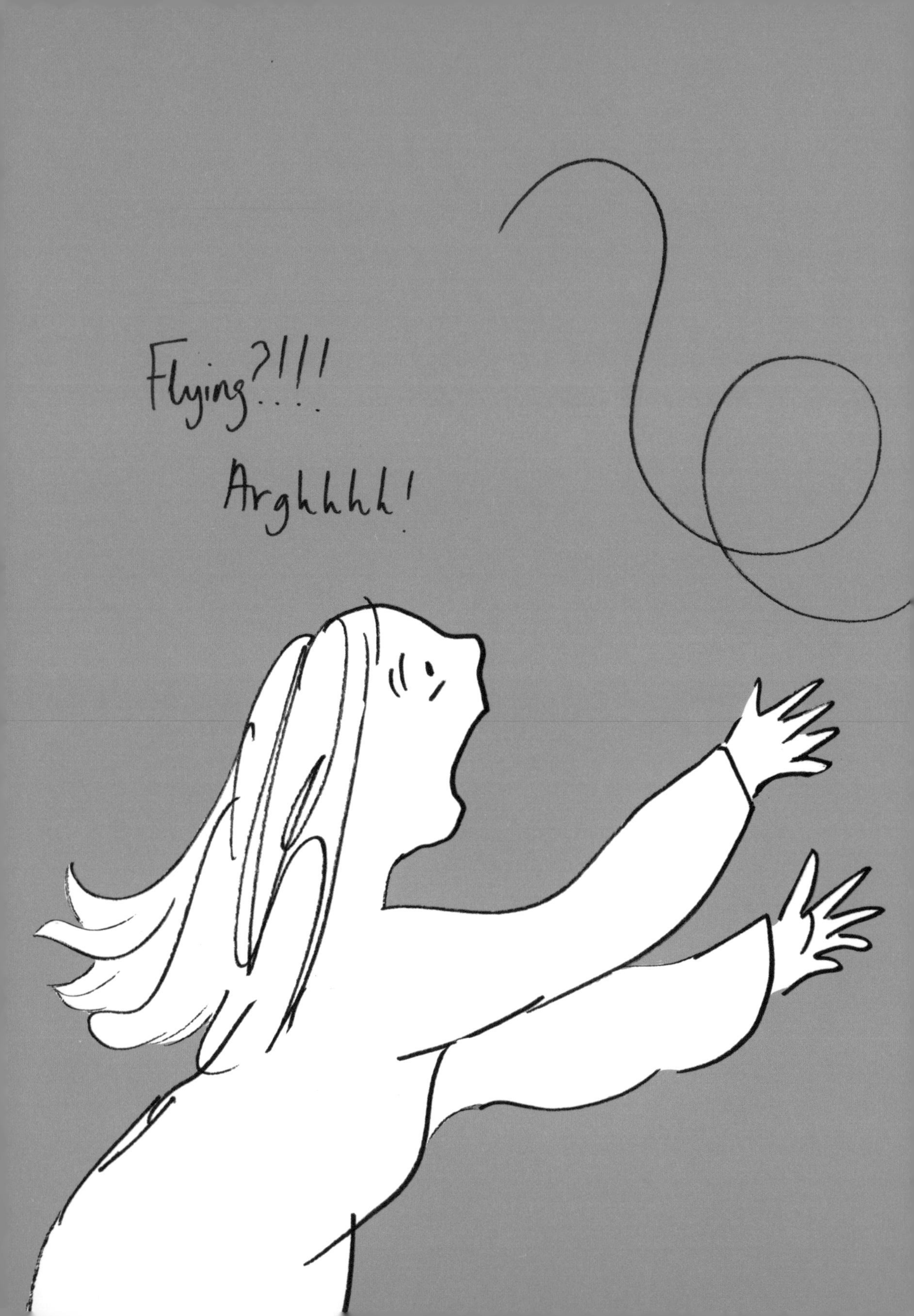
Flying?!!!.....
Arghhhh!

Phase Two

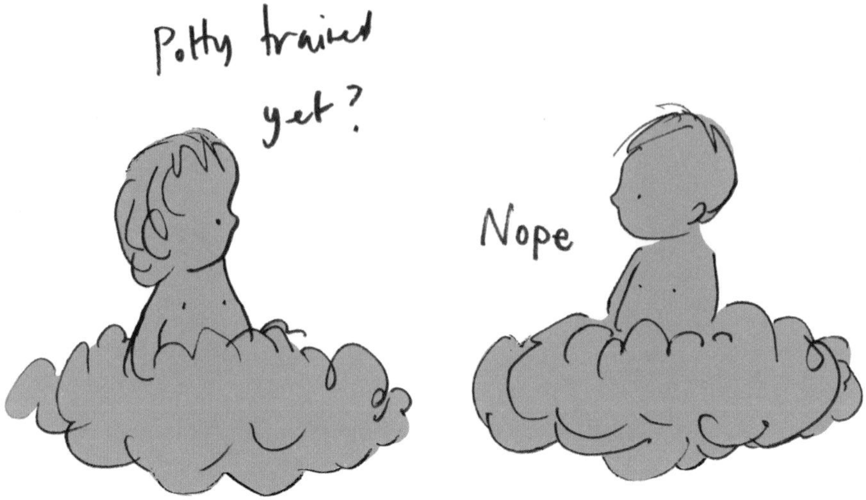
Potty trained yet?
Nope

Jibble wobble
  flibble
Cabble dooble
    woo.

Abblee
  doohee
   flooup
   floup
     pnarrpp.

flibble
jib.

Now you're
talking.

gluggle
fuggle
sulp

slurp.

Tired?

Please sleep.

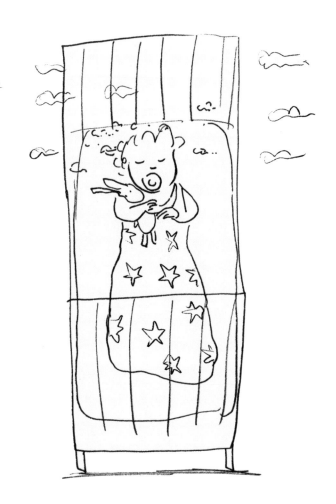

Mumma...

...Mumma?

Mumma?

Mumma!!!

Mumma.

Dadda!

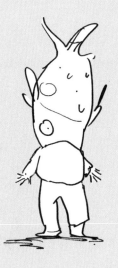

first we wash...

and then...

we dry.

This is where
I draw the line.

Thanks.

I'm sorry I
lost
my
temper,
sweetheart.

S'ok
Mumma.

Me time...

You time...

Take home, Mumma?

Take home, Mumma?

Take home, Mumma?

Take home, Mumma

Take
home, Mumma

Gentle.

...Be gentle. Please.

That's not gentle.

No cuddles.

So humiliating.

Somebody... HELP ME!

Oh, hello, baby dinosaur.

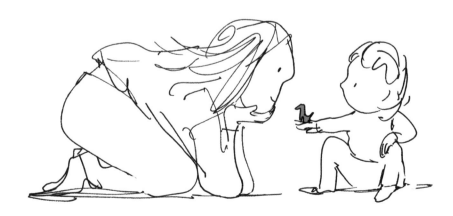

Carry me
carry me
Carry me

wait

wait

wait

got you
got you
got you

please sleep.

Phase Three

Mom?

Mom?

Mom?

Mom?

Mom?

Mom?

Booger.

Thanks, Mom.

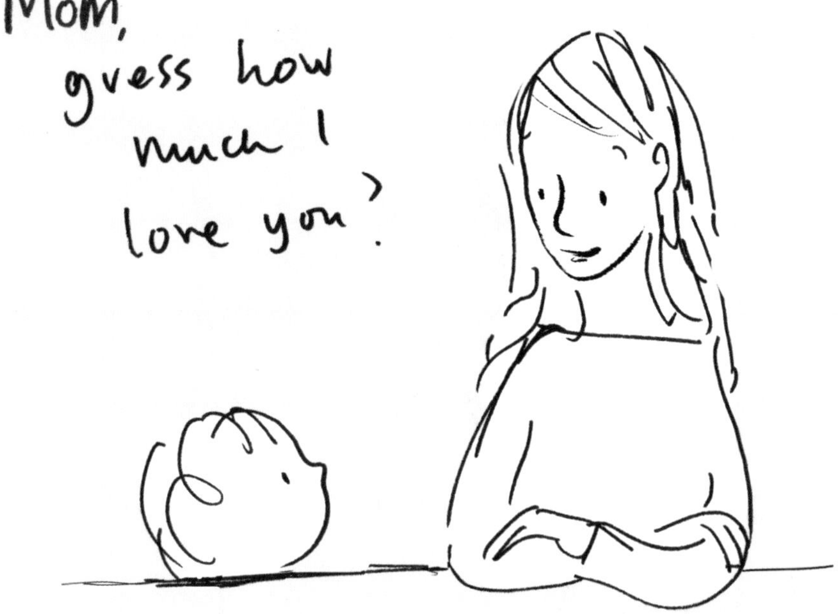

Oh. I don't think I can.

I love you all the way
to the kitchen ...

... and back again.

Wow, that's a lot!

And I love you too.

... all the way

to the kitchen...

... and back again.

Mom,
why are
you
crying?

Because
your
shoes
are so
small.

Wow.
Grown-ups
are
weird.

Pee pee, Mom.

My
ball is
too
yucky.

My
ball is
too
Stripy.

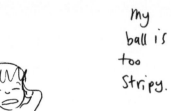

My ball is too ball-y.

My
ball
is too...

...gone.

Poo poo.

Where?

Choo
choo
poo
poo

 Why?

 Why?

 Why?

 Why?

 Why?

 Why?

Just...

...because.

Yuck.

Yuck.

YUCK.

Yuck.

Y-U-C-K.

Yuck. Yuck. Yuck.

YUCK!!

Yum!

Please
sleep.

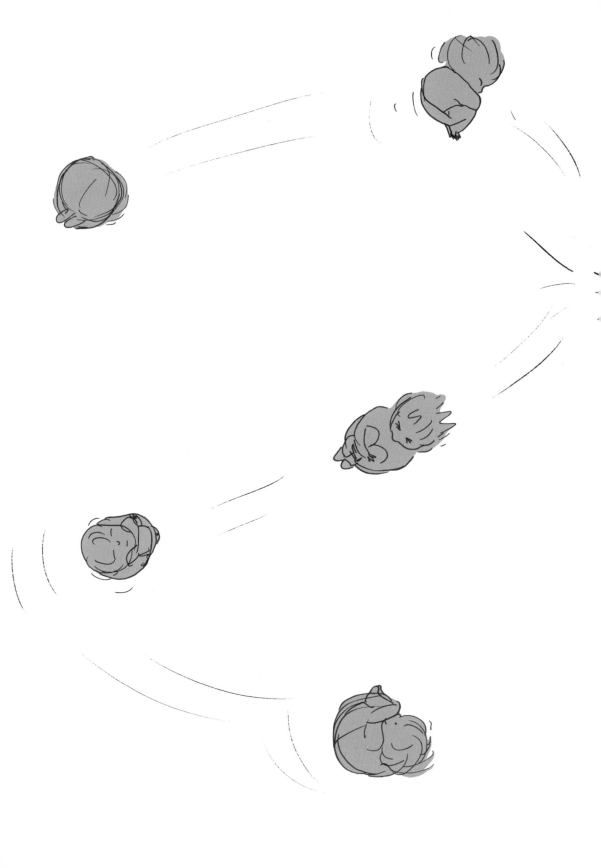

Morning!

Too early?

No.

Tea, Dad?

There go,

Look, Mom.

Look, Mom.

Look. Mom.

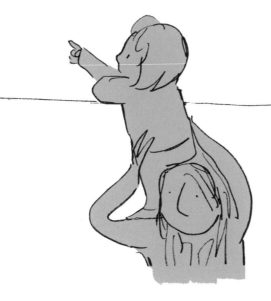

Do you see,

Mom?

Wow,

Mom.

Poo

poo.

Me keep for ever.

Mom

Mom

Mom

Mom

Mom

Mom

Mom

Mom

Mom

Mom

Mom

Mom

Mom

This is nice.

Please,
please,
please
sleep.

what's that noise?

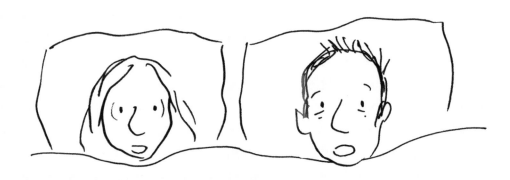

Silence?

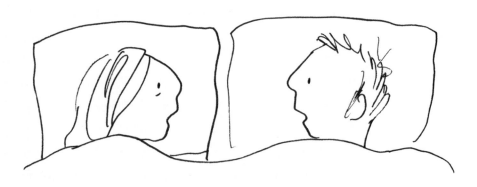

HE SLEPT!!!

He slept!
He slept!
He slept!

He slept
all night long!

Let's
have
another
one!

Phase Four

Doesn't look
very wonderful
to me.

Hey Mom, did you swallow the moon?

that's a
bit greedy.

I'd rather have
cheese puffs.

meet
your
brother.

It's just
a phase.

Phase Five

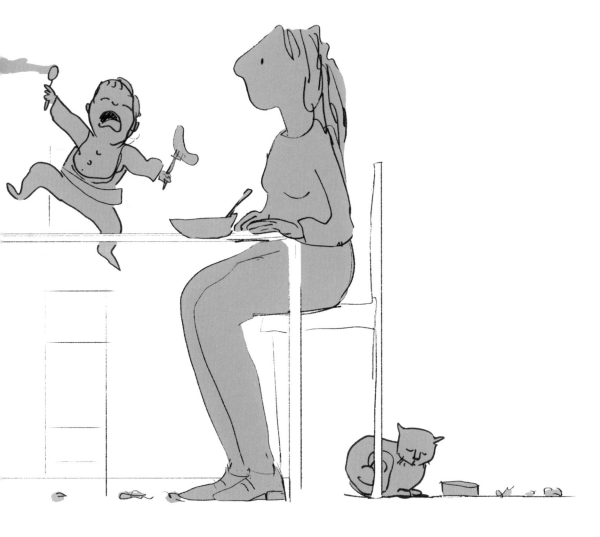

Row, Row, Row

your boat

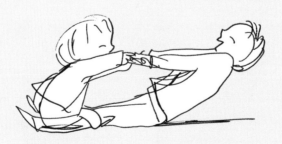

gently down the stream,

merrily, merrily, merrily, merrily,

...life is but a dream.

Let it
all wash
over
you.

Look to the light.

Love.

Live.

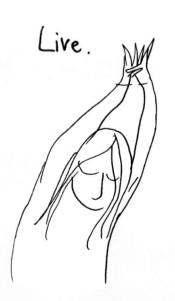

Breathe.

Be.

Drink ALL the coffee.

...and if that doesn't work?

Hide.

(Somewhere better than this.)

Shall we go home now?

Hey Mom, cant you draw
something funny?

BLAST OFF!!!

1..

2..

3..

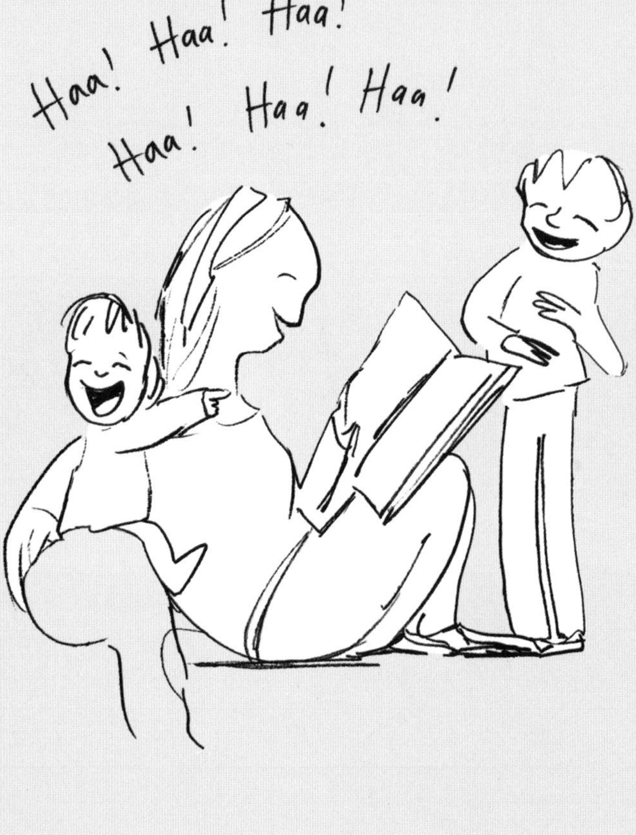
Haa! Haa! Haa!
Haa! Haa! Haa!

Washing the dishes.

Drying the dishes.

Juggling the dishes.

Spinning the dishes.

Dropping the dishes.

Throwing the dishes...

Sweeping the dishes.

Forget the
dishes.

... ordering delivery.

Mom, are you
hiding again?

Sleep, please.

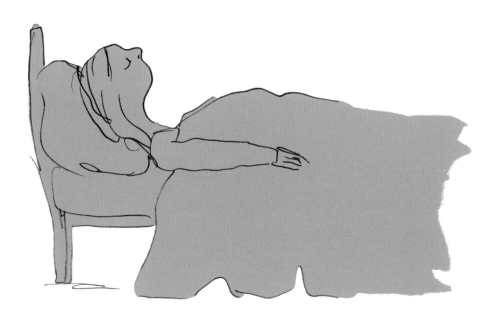

Yes, dears?

Phase Six

There's no toilet paper! Actually...

...don't worry, Mom... I can reach the curtain...

...All clean now!

I'd give
you the
moon,

I'd give you
the stars,

I'd give you the
whole, wide
world

and all the
beauty in it.

what's
that?

No, I won't give
you a cookie.

Is anyone going to feed me?

Last time I looked
I was twenty-five.

Maybe if
I just fix
my hair...

... Some earrings....

...A smidge of make-up...

Great.

I've still got it.

I'm
going
out!

Me do it.

One leg...

two legs...

...and pull.

Ta - dah ...

Good to go!

Me time...

You time.

I quite like
this phase.

Weeeeeee!

Don't worry, love.
Preschool will
be great and
you'll be
absolutely
fine.

Bye!

Bye!

Love you.

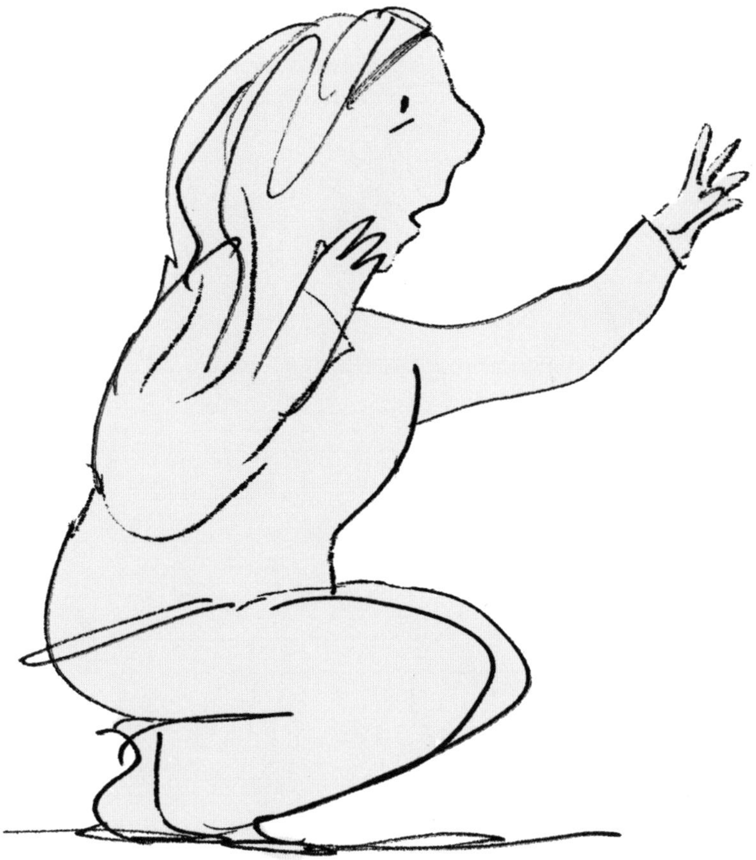

Bye.

... absolutely fine.

How was preschool?

First I stood
like this.

Then I peeped
like this.

I was brave and
waved like this.

And flapped a bit...

like this.

Soon I was flying,
like this.

Sounds great!

...And then
what
happened?

This.

Hey, Dad !

Wow, Mom.

Er, Mom.
There's some

IMAGINATION

in the laundry
basket...

Phase Seven

and it's looking
at us.

Please put your shoes on.

Put your shoes on.

Are you listening!?

I SAID...

...PUT YOUR SHOES ON!!

Mom! Quick!

Thanks.

hhhhhhhhh

We're
not going
anywhere until
you're calmed
down.

That's
more
like it.

Now let's
try and have
a nice day.

There
is a
monster.

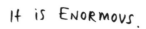

... Has a big
hairy-scary
bum ... like this,

It stomps like
this.

...and when it's
angry..

ROAR!

But that's
ok
'cos everyone
knows...

...even monsters...

... just
need
love.

I
said
donut.

where is
my donut.

Is anyone even listening?

Does anyone even care...

... about donuts.

Giddy-up, horsey!

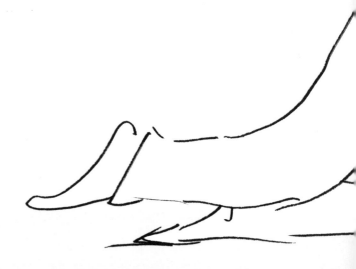

This phase
is fun.

Look, here comes Archibald...

Hi, Archie!!

He was just a caterpillar.

Look at him now!

Wow.

I'm going to
be a butterfly
when I grow up.

Me too.

Can't you see I'm busy.

...But
Mom!!

The laundry is

getting out of hand.

what's up, honey?

Tiredy-pops?

Grumpy-wumpy?

Pants-problem?

Drinky-winky?

Cookie-wookie?

cuddle-wuddle-woo-woo?

Mom, do you mind...

I'm just thinking.

Sit, Mumma.

Stay.

Fetch,

Mumma.

Good, Mumma.

Lunch?

... Can't you see
we're busy.

I need some
thing.

Thanks.

Got any
card board ?

Brilliant.

Thanks.

Toilet paper rolls?

Marvelous.

I need your chair.

I'm taking your desk and laptop too.

Anything
else
you
need?

Phase Eight

To the moon,
of course!

So, to sum up...

Motherhood is...

breath-taking

mind-blowing

eye-popping

totally
tiring

Sometimes
frightening

endlessly
inspiring

unrelenting

metamorphosing

quite astonishing

mind-numbing

soul-shaking

impossibly
exasperating

heart-expanding

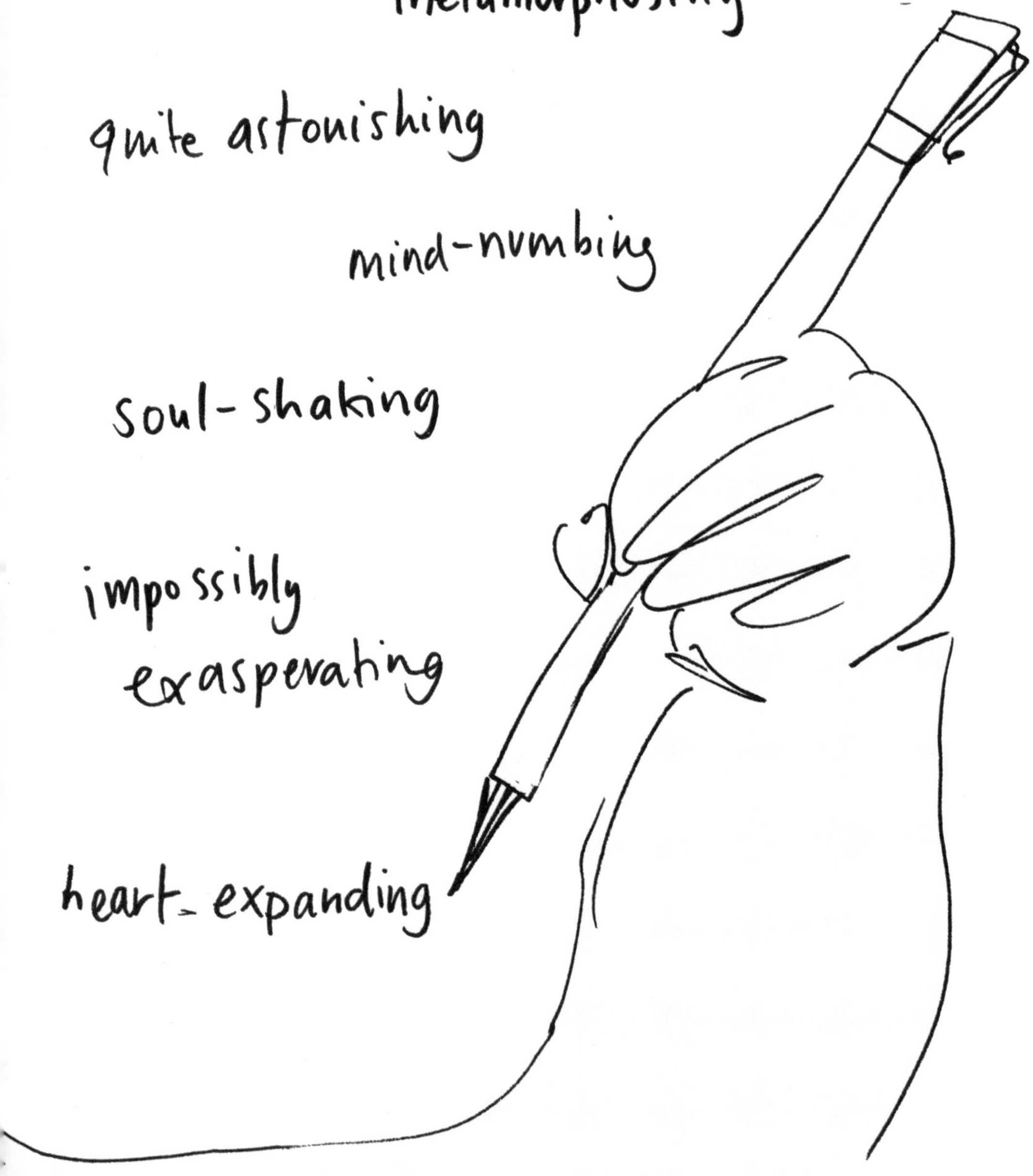

...and a
Magical,
beautiful
privilege.

Have you finished
yet, Mom?

Yes.

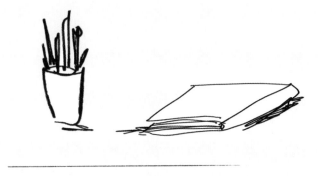

Good.

We need
your
pens.

THe END

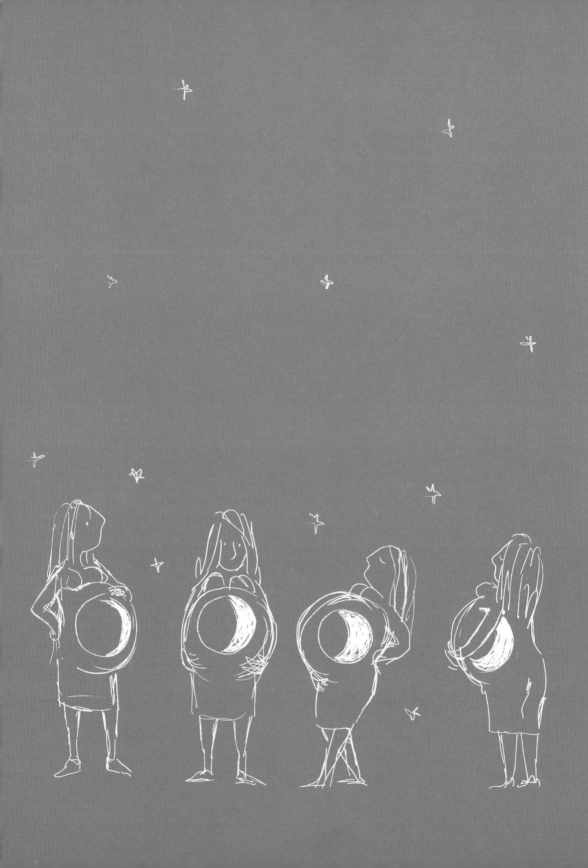